me and my piano
part 1

very first lessons for the young pianist

with

Fanny Waterman
and
Marion Harewood

Faber Music Ltd
London

Dear **Nathanael**

We are so glad you are going to learn to play the piano. The rainbow colours:

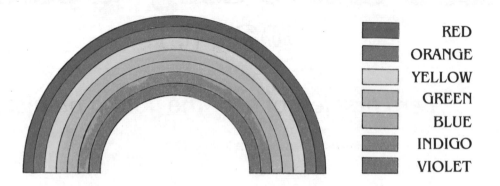

RED
ORANGE
YELLOW
GREEN
BLUE
INDIGO
VIOLET

will help you find the notes on the piano and on the music. In this book you'll meet many new friends – Postman Pete, the Ostrich and his friends at the Zoo, the Caterpillar, and the Old Man with the Beard – as well as some old favourites such as Mary and her little lamb, and Old Macdonald. There are some exciting puzzles and games to work out, and when you finish the book, your teacher will sign your certificate. We do hope that you and your piano will have lots of fun together.

Fanny Waterman

and

Marion Harewood

Teachers and Parents

- Note names are identified with colours to assist note-learning, without involving colour-coded notation in the music. Matching coloured stickers on the piano keys may be found helpful in the early stages.

© Faber Music Ltd 1988

First published in 1988 by Faber Music Ltd,
3 Queen Square London WC1N 3AU

Music drawn by Sheila Stanton
Designed and illustrated by Julia Osorno
Cover typography by Julia Osorno

Typeset by Bookworm Typesetting Ltd, Manchester

Printed in England by Reflex Litho

Always

- Play with clean hands and short fingernails.

- Check that the chair or piano stool is in the middle of the keyboard and at the right height.

- Make sure you are sitting correctly.

- Play with curved fingers, like this:

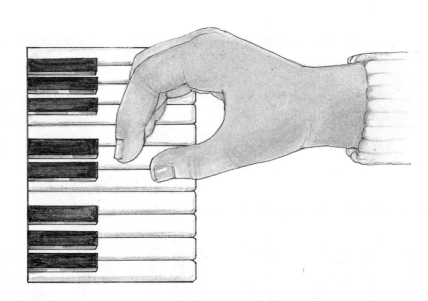

- Use the same fingering every time you play a piece.

- Listen to every sound you make on the piano.

The Piano Keyboard

middle of piano

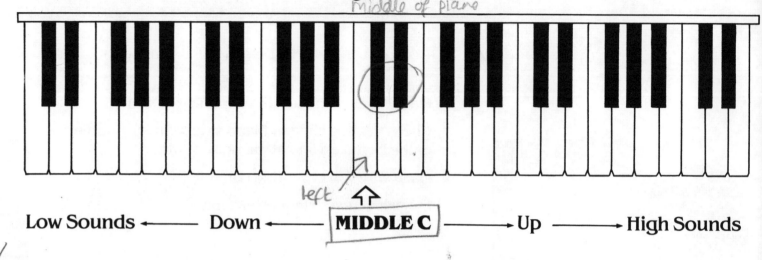

left

Low Sounds ← — Down ← — **MIDDLE C** → Up — → High Sounds

The piano keyboard has **white** and **black** notes.   The **black** notes are in groups of 2's and 3's.

Find the group of 2 **black** notes nearest to the middle.   The **white** note to the left of them is called **Middle C.**

28th Feb

- *find middle c* ✓
- *jump up all the Cs* ✓ *and back down again*
- *jump up all the As Bs Ds* ✓ *etc.*
- *3 blind mice*

Imagine you are a frog hopping up the keyboard

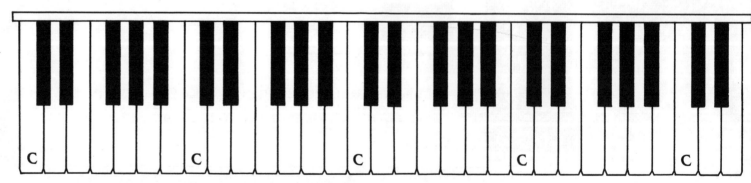

Find all the C notes on the keyboard.

Then play every C note from the bottom to the top, hopping like a frog from one to the next.

The Musical Rainbow

The musical alphabet has seven letters, just as the rainbow has seven colours.

These seven letters are repeated all the way up the piano keyboard.

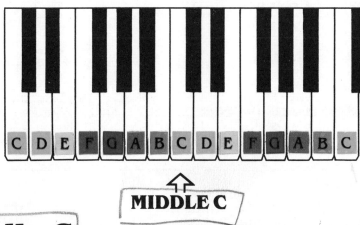

C D E F G A B C D E F G A B C

↑
MIDDLE C

Find Middle C

From there, climb up the Musical Rainbow, naming each note as you go.
At the top, play another C, then go back down, naming each note.

Frog Hops

Play every D from the bottom to the top. Then every E, then F, G, A, and B.
Now you are back to C!

Three Blind Mice

Here are the first notes of Three Blind Mice.
Play them on the piano.

Practice =

EDC EDC GFE GFE

Word Game

Can you play these words?

BAG   CAB   BEE   BED   FACE

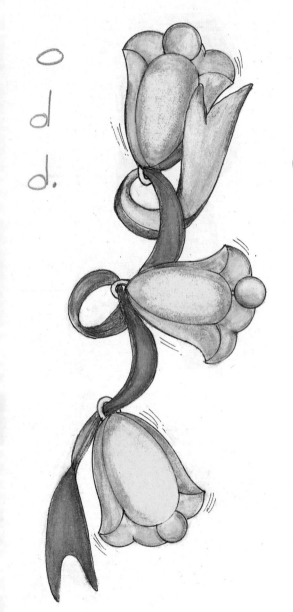

Counting the Time

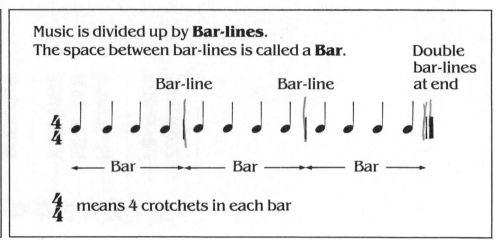

$\bullet$ = 1 beat = **Crotchet**

$\bullet$ = 2 beats = **Minim**

$\circ$ = 4 beats = **Semibreve**

Music is divided up by **Bar-lines**.
The space between bar-lines is called a **Bar**.

Double bar-lines at end

Bar-line   Bar-line

←— Bar —→←— Bar —→←— Bar —→

$\frac{4}{4}$ means 4 crotchets in each bar

Clap these rhythms, counting aloud to 4.   The notes marked > should have an **accent**.   Play them louder than the others.

Teacher: turn these into duets by clapping crotchets.

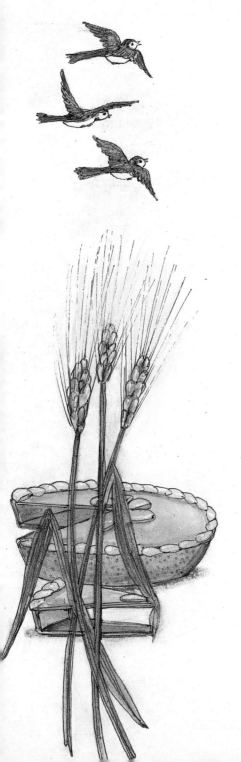

> Clap the time, saying the words aloud.
> Now, say the words again, playing Middle C at the same time.

Yankee Doodle

Yan-kee Doo-dle   went to town   ri - ding   on a   po - ny.

Stuck a   fea-ther   in his hat and   called it   ma-ca-   ro - ni.

Sing a Song of Sixpence

Sing   a   song of   six - pence, a   pock-et full of   rye,

Four and twen-ty black - birds   baked   in a   pie;

When the pie was   o - pened, the   birds be-gan to   sing,

Was-n't   that a   dain - ty dish to   set be-fore a   king?

Finding the Way from the Music

1 Music is written on a **stave** or **staff**.
It has five lines with spaces between.

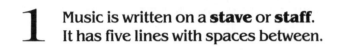

2 Notes are written on the **lines**
or in the **spaces**.

line notes

space notes

3 High notes are written in the
Treble Clef.

right hand

4 **Middle C** has its very own line.
In the Treble Clef it is below the stave.

5 The Right Hand plays high notes.

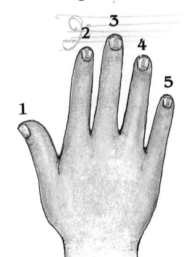

Hold up your Right Hand

Point to your 3rd finger.
Point to your 1st finger.
Point to your 5th finger.
Point to your 2nd finger.
Point to your 4th finger.

Going to the Zoo

Clap the rhythm, then play.

Kangaroo

We are go-ing to the zoo. We will see the Kan-ga-roo.

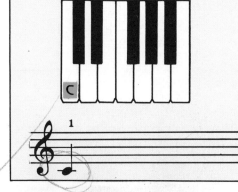

New note C

Crocodile

Cro-co-dile, How you smile, If you move I'll run a mile.

Bears

Practice this one 7·3·02

Bears, bears in their ca-ges. Black Bear, how he ra-ges,

Hear him growl, See him scowl, He wants his tea, Like you and me.

Middle D, Middle C

Postman Pete

Postman Pete Accompaniment

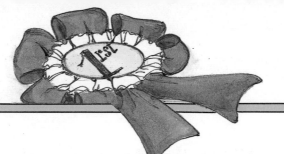

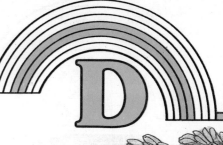

$\frac{2}{4}$ means 2 crotchets in the bar.

At the piano

Let's be - gin my mu - sic les - son, I can now play C D C.

My Pony

Trot - ting on my po - ny, She's a lit - tle dap - ple grey.

Hope we'll win some pri - zes at the Po - ny Club to - day.

My Pony Accompaniment

d = 2   d. = 3   d = 1   d. = 3   d.   d = 1
. = 1   d.   d = 2   . = ½
                    o = 4   d. = 1½

E

3rd finger

New note E

C D E

1 2 3

This is E   *Practice 14·3·02*

1 2 3   2 1 2   3 2 1 2 3 2 1

This is E.   This is D.   Up and down from E to C.

Practice I can jump - using 5 notes/5 fingers UP & DOWN = lift up fingers so you can only hear one note at a time

This sign :| at the end of a piece is a Repeat sign. It means play the piece again.

Telephone   *Practice 14·3·02*

E 3   2   3   2   3 2 1

1 Te - le - phone.   It's for me.   Grand-ma's ask - ing us to tea.
2 We'll have chips,   we'll have cake,   We'll have ice-cream on a plate.

Telephone Accompaniment

12   New Note E

Sammy Squirrel

Practice 21.3.02

Sam-my Squir-rel up a tree, Climbs the bran-ches ea-si-ly.

Sam-my, please come down the tree, back to me.

Fingering
Use next-door fingers for next-door notes.
A note left out means a finger left out.

A dot after a note increases its length by half.

♩. = 3 beats = **Dotted Minim** (♩ + ♪)

The Ostrich

Practice 21.3.02

Words by May Wilkins Freer

The os-trich is a sil-ly bird with scarce-ly a-ny mind. He

of-ten runs so ve-ry fast he leaves him-self be-hind.

Sammy Squirrel and The Ostrich Accompaniment

F

New note F

C D E F

1 2 3 4

Good night, good morning

2 3 1   2 3 4 3   2 3 1

Close your eyes   for the night.   We will wake up when it's light.

Snowflakes | Practice 21·3·02

4 3 4 1   2 4 1   2 3 4 1   2 3 4

Snow-flakes gent - ly swirl - ing round, fal - ling soft - ly to the ground.

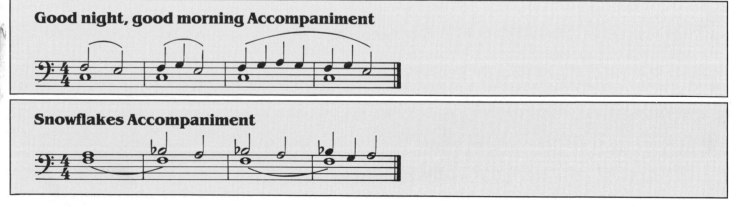

Good night, good morning Accompaniment

Snowflakes Accompaniment

14   New Note F

Tunes can start on any beat of the bar.
This one starts on the 4th beat.

The Railway Train

The rail - way train is start - ing off, The en - gine gives a

migh - ty cough. The whis - tle blows, the sig - nal shows, The

guard says 'Right' and off it goes.

The Railway Train Accompaniment

New note G

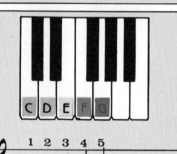

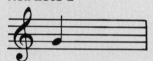

Escalator

Up and down the es-ca-la-tor, hav-ing lots of fun.

Thought it all a great big joke till scol-ded by my mum.

Jelly on a plate

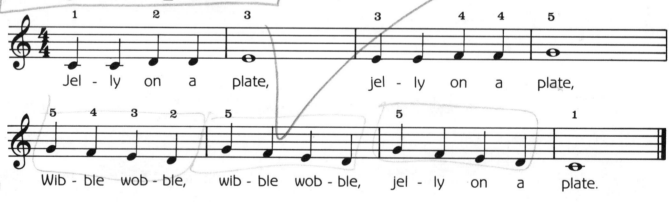

Jel-ly on a plate, jel-ly on a plate,

Wib-ble wob-ble, wib-ble wob-ble, jel-ly on a plate.

Jelly on a plate Accompaniment

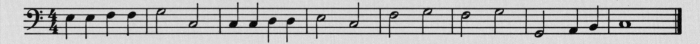

18th April 02
• I can jump
• Mary had a little lamb
• Bo-peep.
• Treble clefs

The Pancake

Words by Christina Rossetti

Mix a pan-cake, stir a pan-cake, pop it in the pan.

Fry the pan-cake, toss the pan-cake, catch it if you can.

Mary had a little lamb

1 Ma - ry had a lit - tle lamb, lit - tle lamb, lit - tle lamb.
2 Ev' - ry - where that Ma - ry went, Ma - ry went, Ma - ry went,

Ma - ry had a lit - tle lamb, its fleece was white as snow.
Ev' - ry - where that Ma - ry went the lamb was sure to go.

The Pancake Accompaniment

Mary had a little lamb Accompaniment

Three in a Bar

$\frac{3}{4}$ means 3 crotchets in each bar.

Clap these rhythms, counting aloud to 3.

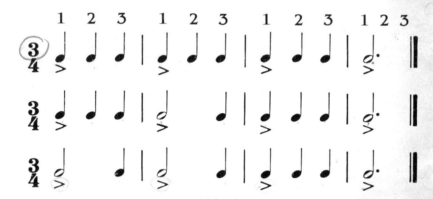

Teacher: turn these into duets by clapping crotchets.

Humpty Dumpty

Clap the time, saying the words aloud.

$\frac{3}{4}$ Hump – ty Dump – ty sat on a wall.

Hump – ty Dump – ty had a great fall.

All the king's hor-ses and all the king's men,

Could-n't put Hump-ty to - ge-ther a - gain.

Little Bo-Peep 19

Monkey Puzzles 1

Write in the names of these notes.

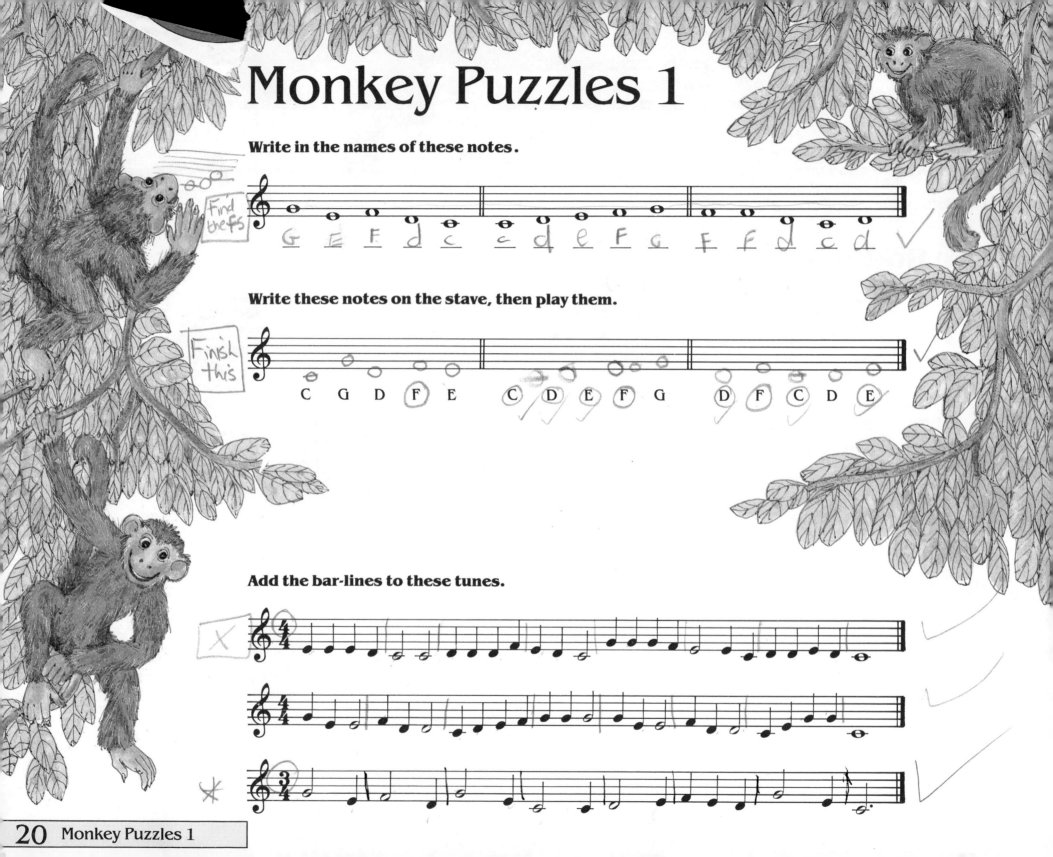

G E F c c d e F G F F d c d

Write these notes on the stave, then play them.

C G D F E   C D E F G   D F C D E

Add the bar-lines to these tunes.

Play these words:

FED   EGG   EDGE

Copy more treble clefs. ...more at home.

♩	= 1 beat = crotchet
♩	= 2 beats = minim
♩.	= 3 beats = dotted minim
o	= 4 beats = semibreve

How many beats in each note?

| 4 | 4 | 3 | 4 | 2 | 1 | 1 | 4 |

How many beats to each bar?

| 4 | 3 | 4 | 3 | 2 |

Write these notes:

Semibreve G   Minim D   Dotted Minim F   Crotchet C   Minim E

25.4.02
• I can jump with left hand
• Girls and boys come out to play
• Monkeys
• What is your name
• Monkey Puzzles 2 — as marked *

Girls and Boys come out to play

Girls and boys come out to play, the moon doth shine as bright as day. Leave your sup-pers and leave your sleep, and come with your play-fel-lows in the street.

Girls and Boys Accompaniment

The Left Hand

1 Low notes are written in the **Bass Clef**.

2 **Middle C** has its own line.
In the Bass Clef it is above the stave.

3 The Left Hand plays low notes.

Hold up your Left Hand.
Point to your 3rd finger.
Point to your 1st finger.
Point to your 5th finger.
Point to your 2nd finger.
Point to your 4th finger.

Left Hand Middle C

Mid - dle   C   Left   Hand   play - ing   Mid - dle   C.

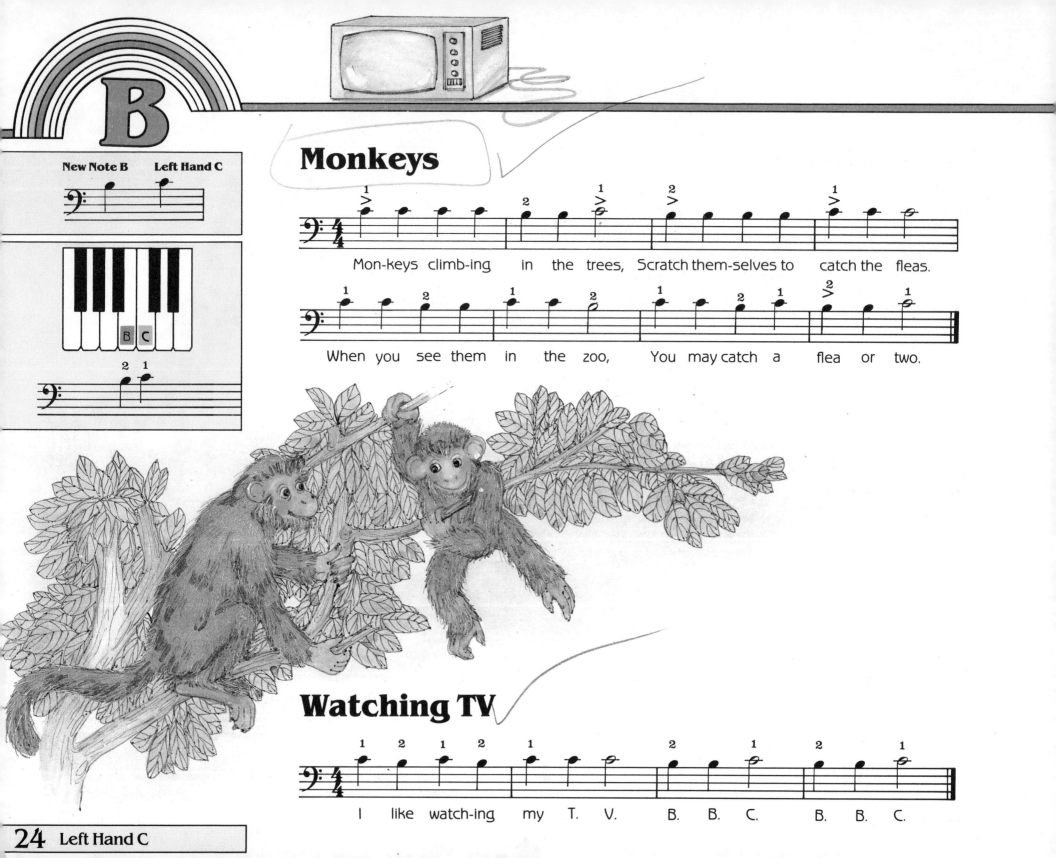

B

New Note B   **Left Hand C**

Monkeys

Mon-keys climb-ing in the trees, Scratch them-selves to catch the fleas.

When you see them in the zoo, You may catch a flea or two.

Watching TV

I like watch-ing my T. V. B. B. C. B. B. C.

The Caterpillar

Ca - ter - pil - lar   crawl-ing round.   His   8   feet make not   a   sound.

What is your name?

What   is   your   name?   Gem - ma   or   Jane?

Don't   tell   me   now,   I'll   ask   you   a - gain.

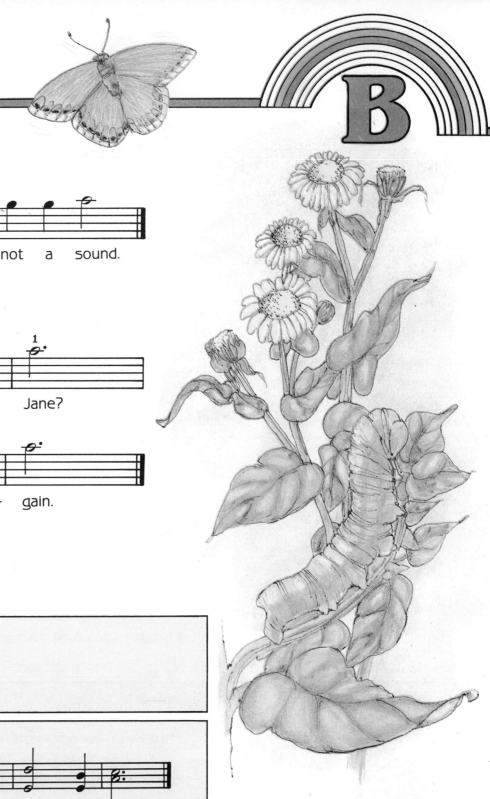

The Caterpillar Accompaniment

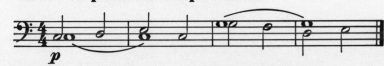

What is your name? Accompaniment

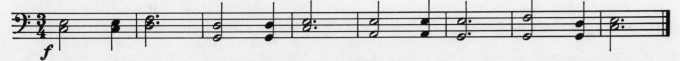

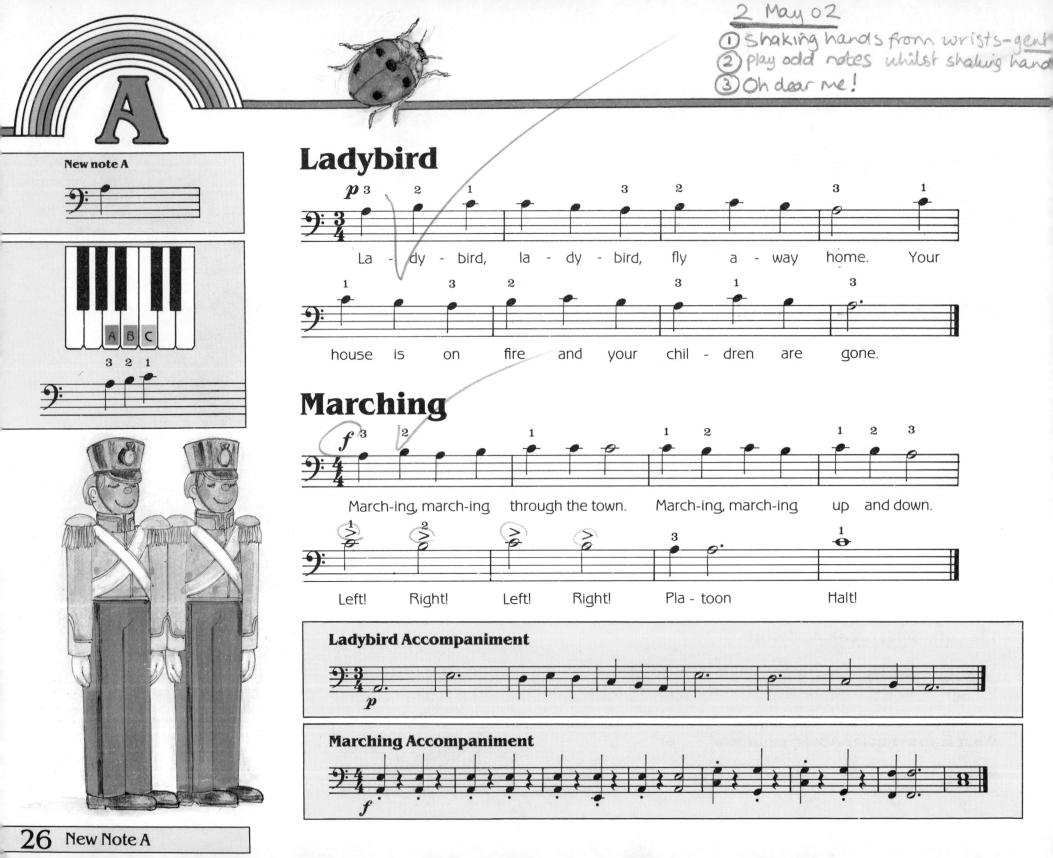

Ladybird

Ladybird, ladybird, fly away home. Your house is on fire and your children are gone.

Marching

March-ing, march-ing through the town. March-ing, march-ing up and down.

Left! Right! Left! Right! Pla-toon Halt!

Ladybird Accompaniment

Marching Accompaniment

Oh dear me!

Oh   dear   me!   I'm   not   tall.

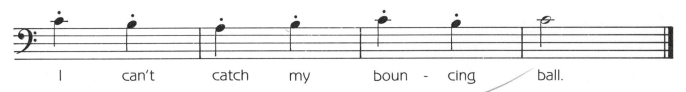

I   can't   catch   my   boun - cing   ball.

Who's that knocking?

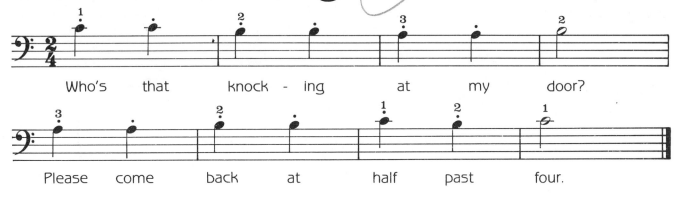

Who's   that   knock - ing   at   my   door?

Please   come   back   at   half   past   four.

Oh dear me! Accompaniment

Who's that knocking? Accompaniment

Staccato

A dot placed over or under a note makes it short and crisp.
Play with a loose wrist like a bouncing ball.

G

New note G

This is C, this is G

This   is   C,   this   is   G,   C   G   C   G   back   to   C.

The Squirrel

The   squir - rel   ran   up,   and   then   he   ran   down,

Up   a - gain,   down   a - gain,   then   round   and   round.

The Squirrel Accompaniment

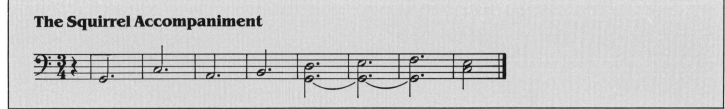

✓ I can jump - 2 hands - try in different places on the piano

✓ I am the prince

✓ See-saw with p of
The robin   quite soft   and ✓ Bugle call

mp	= *mezzo-piano* = moderately soft
mf	= *mezzo-forte* = moderately loud

quite loud.

I am the Prince

I   am   the   Prince,   hap - py   and   free.

This   is   a   waltz,   come   dance   with   me.

I am the Prince Accompaniment

New note F

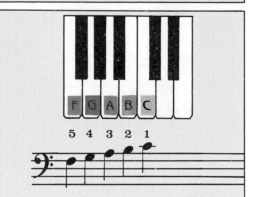

Running down to F

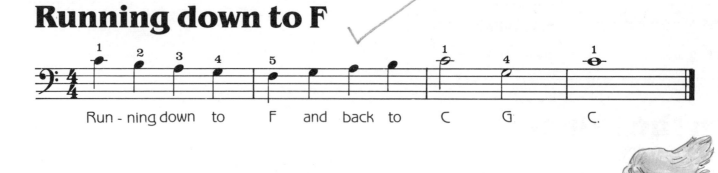

Run - ning down to F and back to C G C.

See-Saw

p Up, down, up, down on the see - saw, We can touch the sky!

f Bob - by likes to bump the ground, Jen - ny likes to fly!

The Robin

staccato

mf Lit - tle Ro - bin Red - breast sat up - on a tree.

When I threw him bread - crumbs, he flew down to me.

Bugle Call

f Ta - ra ta - ra boom-de ay, Hear the bug - le call to - day.

Two Hands

ALL WITH 2 HANDS

16.5.02
• The Spaceman
• Westminster chimes
• I can jump <>
• Jungle Drums - 2 hands

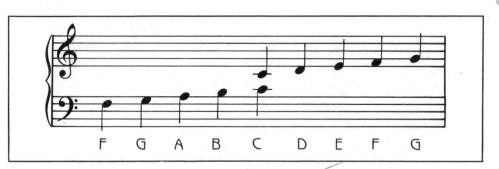

F G A B C D E F G

The Spaceman

f Space-man walk-ing on the moon, Don't fall off now! Come down soon.

Westminster Chimes

Teacher: now play the chord

Jungle Drums

Rowing

If two notes of the same pitch are joined by a curve

this is called a **tie**.

Play the first note and hold it on for the value of the second note.

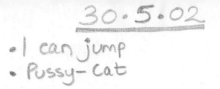

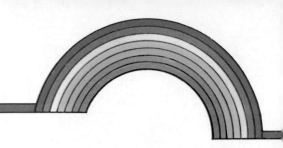

30.5.02
• I can jump
• Pussy-Cat

Pussy-Cat

3 TIME

Pus - sy cat, pus - sy cat, where have you been? I've
been up to Lon - don to vis - it the Queen.
Pus - sy cat, pus - sy cat, what did you there? I
fright - ened a lit - tle mouse un - der her chair. Mee - ow.

Monkey Puzzles 2

ke-s

Write in these notes:

*finish

D   F   E   C   G   F   D   C

B   G   F   A   C   G   A   F

Copy more Bass Clefs if time

A Musical Crossword

Across

4 Note with 4 beats
5 The clef for the Left Hand
6 Getting louder
10 *Diminuendo* means getting . . . . .

Down

1 Notes with 2 beats
2 The clef for the Right Hand
3 They're black and white
4 The name for dots over the notes
7 The sign at the beginning of a stave
8 What Middle C (or D, or E) is
9 The number of finger you would use
   to play C in either hand

Answers on p. 49

A Quiz

Write your answers in the spaces and then play them on the piano

Where you go to sleep _Bed_ ✓

A furry insect that stings _Bee_ ✓

A green vegetable _cabbage_ ✓

What Humpty Dumpty was _egg_ ✓

Hard of hearing _deaf_ ✓

A lot of these make a necklace _bead_ ✓

Father _Dad_ ✓

dead

Can you make up some more words on the piano?

Yankee Doodle

1 Fill in the missing notes marked * with their proper time-values.
2 Put in the bar-lines.
3 Now play **Yankee Doodle**.

Rests

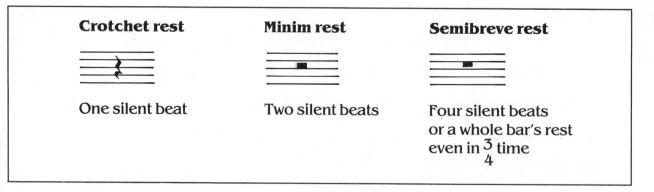

Crotchet rest	Minim rest	Semibreve rest
One silent beat	Two silent beats	Four silent beats or a whole bar's rest even in $\frac{3}{4}$ time

Clap the notes, counting the beats aloud

Old MacDonald

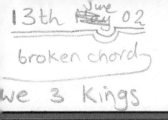

13th June 02
broken chord
we 3 Kings
Laughing clown

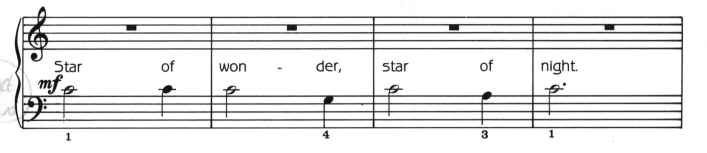

mf Star of won - der, star of night.

1   4   3   1

Star with ro - yal beau - ty bright.

1   4   3   1

1   3   2   3
West - ward lead - ing, still pro - ceed - ing,

p Guide us to thy per - fect light.

1   4   1   3   1

20.6.02
- C chromatic scale ✓
- We 3 Kings
(- Down by the lakeside) — if you've got time.

The Laughing Clown

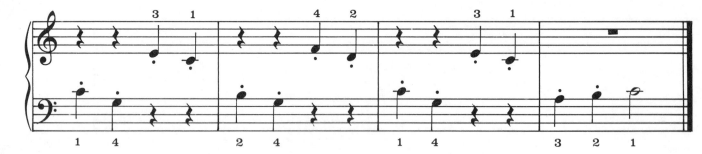

Musical Detective:

1 How many bars are there in the piece? How many beats in each bar?
2 What do the dots under the notes mean?
3 How many crotchet rests are there?
4 How many notes does the Left Hand play?
5 Is the piece loud, moderately loud or soft?
6 Make up your own words for the piece.

My clock

Lis - ten to the tick - tock, tick - tock, tick - tock,

Lis - ten to the tick - tock of my clock.

Down by the lake-side

Music by Beethoven

Down by the lake - side, The sun is out to - day, So

let's take a pic - nic, And all go out to play.

27·6·02
- C chromatic – left hand ✓
- Haunted castle – p, f, etc.
- Saints

Oh when the Saints go marching in

American traditional

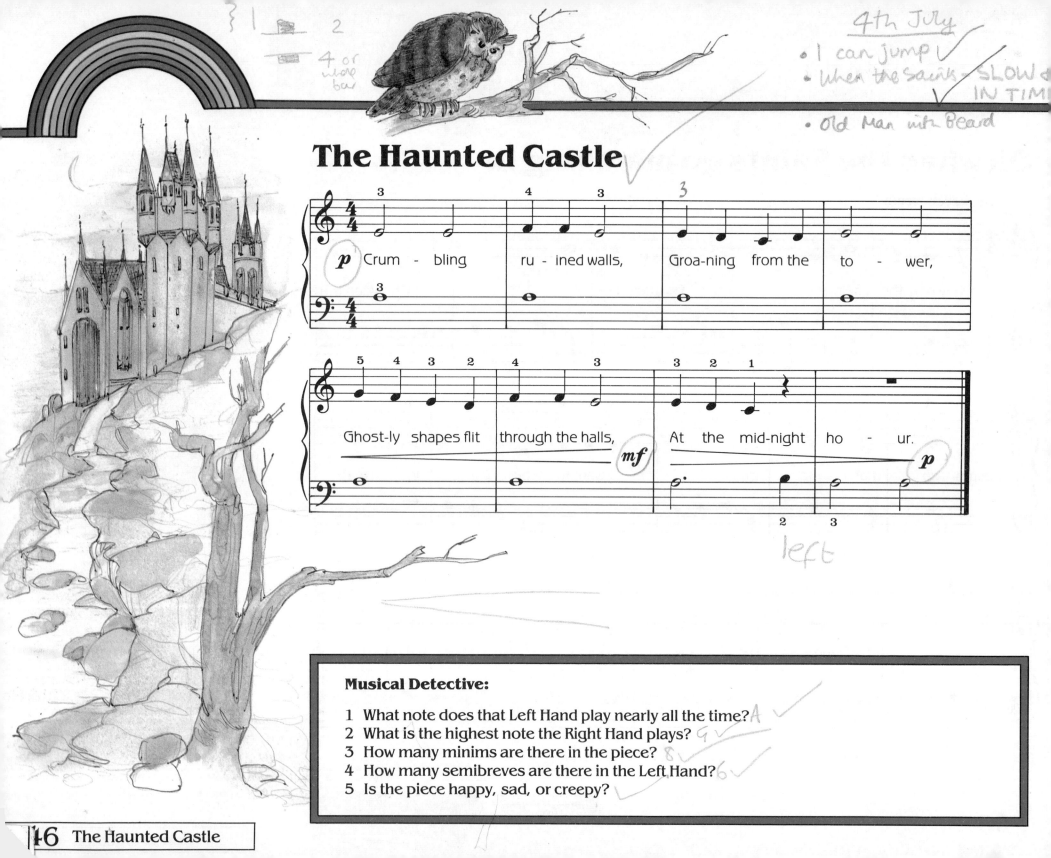

The Haunted Castle

Crum - bling   ru - ined walls,   Groa-ning from the   to - wer,

p

Ghost-ly shapes flit   through the halls,   At   the mid-night   ho - ur.

mf   *p*

Musical Detective:

1 What note does that Left Hand play nearly all the time?
2 What is the highest note the Right Hand plays?
3 How many minims are there in the piece?
4 How many semibreves are there in the Left Hand?
5 Is the piece happy, sad, or creepy?

11th July
- I can jump ✓
- any old pieces
- old Man with Beard — practise (slowly) for 1st 1/2 of holidays
    — then you can go quicker.

There was an Old Man with a Beard

Words by Edward Lear

12.9.02
- I can jump
- Old Man Beard

mf There was an Old Man with a Be - ard ____ f Who

said, 'It is just as I fe - ared ____ p Two

owls and a hen, Four larks and a wren f Have

all built their nests in my be - ard'.

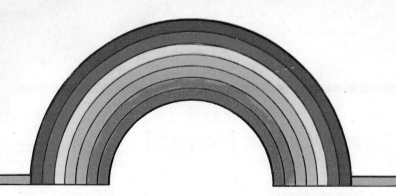

rainbow certificate

This is to certify that

Nathanael Wong

successfully completed

me and my piano   part 1

on

19th September 2002

Congratulations!

Fanny Waterman.

Fanny Waterman

J.S.Cooper.

Teacher's signature

Marion Harewood

Marion Harewood